"Taylor Mac has the smarts to take on the big themes and find credible and incredible arguments in each . . . The language of *Gary* is marked by the play's high style, by its pathos and its rhythm . . . Mac's ability to elevate doggerel to verse is no small thing: it is the work of a real writer expressing depths in a popular form."

—HILTON ALS, *NEW YORKER*

"Expect plenty of fart jokes and penis wagging and doubles entendre interlaced with the sweet humanity and higher-toned political satire . . . There's no shortage of art and craft in this offbeat show."

—MARILYN STASIO, *VARIETY*

"Much of *Gary* is an outrageous mix of the grotesque and the absurd, designed to make audiences gape . . . If staging *Gary* on Broadway is in some sense a folly, it's the kind we could use a lot more of."

—ADAM FELDMAN, *TIME OUT NEW YORK*

"*Gary* is a farce, a piece of messy circus . . . There is nothing like it on Broadway, and that is to be welcomed. It is an argument for art, and a passionate call for resistance." —TIM TEEMAN, *DAILY BEAST*

TAYLOR MAC (who uses "judy"—lowercase [*sic*]—as a gender pronoun) is the author of *Joy and Pandemic*; *The Hang* (composed by Matt Ray); *Gary: A Sequel to Titus Andronicus*; *A 24-Decade History of Popular Music*; *Prosperous Fools*; *The Fre*; *Hir*; *The Walk Across America for Mother Earth*; *The Lily's Revenge*; *The Young Ladies Of*; *Red Tide Blooming*; *The Be(A)st of Taylor Mac*; and the revues *Comparison Is Violence*; *Holiday Sauce*; and *The Last Two People on Earth: An Apocalyptic Vaudeville* (created with Mandy Patinkin, Susan Stroman, and Paul Ford). Mac is the first American to receive the International Ibsen Award; is a MacArthur Fellow, a Pulitzer Prize finalist, a Tony nominee for Best Play; and is the recipient of the Edward M. Kennedy Prize for Drama Inspired by American History (with Matt Ray), the Doris Duke Artist Award, a Guggenheim, the Herb Alpert Award, a Drama League Award, the Helen Merrill Award for Playwriting, the Edwin Booth Award, two Helpmann Awards, a New York Drama Critics' Circle Award, two Obies, two Bessies, and an Ethyl Eichelberger.

GARY

A SEQUEL TO

TITUS ANDRONICUS

TAYLOR MAC

THEATRE COMMUNICATIONS GROUP   NEW YORK   2021

The publication of *Gary: A Sequel to Titus Andronicus* by Taylor Mac, through TCG's Book Program, is made possible in part by the New York State Council on the Arts with the support of the Governor's Office and the New York State Legislature.

TCG books are exclusively distributed to the book trade by Consortium Book Sales and Distribution.

Library of Congress Control Numbers:
2021038158 (print) / 2021038159 (ebook)
ISBN 978-1-55936-982-4 (paperback) / ISBN 978-1-55936-940-4 (ebook)
A catalog record for this book is available from the Library of Congress.

Book design and composition by Lisa Govan
Cover design by Monet Cogbill

Cover art and interior art by Ralph Steadman,
courtesy of DKC/O&M and BLT Communications

First Edition, December 2021
Second Printing, April 2023

Gary is dedicated to my friend,
teacher, colleague, dramaturge,
Fool, and theater mom:
Morgan Jenness

GARY

A SEQUEL TO

TITUS ANDRONICUS

Gary: A Sequel to Titus Andronicus was originally commissioned by HERE Arts Center with the support of The Andrew W. Mellon Foundation's National Playwright Residency Program, administered in partnership with HowlRound.

The original production of *Gary: A Sequel to Titus Andronicus* was produced on Broadway by Scott Rudin, Barry Diller, Eli Bush, Eric Falkenstein, Suzanne Grant, No Guarantees, Universal Theatrical Group, James L. Nederlander, Columbia Live Stage, John Gore Organization, Spring Sirkin, Jay Alix & Una Jackman, Jamie deRoy, Wendy Federman, Barbara Manocherian, Al Nocciolino, Bruce Robert Harris & Jack W. Batman, and Adam Rodner. Executive Producers: Joey Parnes, Sue Wagner, and John Johnson. It opened on April 21, 2019. It was directed by George C. Wolfe. The set design was by Santo Loquasto, the costume design was by Ann Roth, the lighting design was by Jules Fisher and Peggy Eisenhauer, the sound design was by Dan Moses Schreier, the original music was by Danny Elfman, the movement direction was by Bill Irwin. The production stage manager was William Joseph Barnes. The cast was as follows:

CAROL	Julie White
GARY	Nathan Lane
JANICE	Kristine Nielsen

The setting is the opulent banquet room of General Titus Andronicus, post-slaughter and coup. There are levels. The banquet room is light, majestic, and uncluttered in its design, so that the onslaught of clutter from the corpses looks ridiculously out of place inside of it.

There are at least two entrances/exits. There is a makeshift workstation (or two) where bodies are dissected.

The end of the play reveals a Rube Goldberg–like machine made from the slaughter. It is one of the more spectacular moments ever to be seen in the history of theater.

CAROL: A midwife.
GARY: A clown, who becomes a maid, who dreams of being a Fool.
JANICE: A maid.
BABY: A real baby. Son of Aaron and Tamora. A visibly dark-skinned baby.

Gary and Janice speak in slightly overdone British cockney accents. The vernacular is not accurately cockney but an American's playfulness in writing cockney. Carol uses an RP (the non-posh version) and Janice and Gary use an East End London cockney (try not to fall into parody; walk the line between realism and awareness).

There is the appearance of at least one thousand corpses on the stage (a painted backdrop or other theatrical techniques that give the illusion of one thousand corpses may be used; still there should be at least a few hundred three-dimensional corpses). The corpses are soldiers, senators, tribunes, and civilians. They are separated into three mounds: An uncovered large mound at least fourteen feet high, which takes up a third of the stage and consists of clothed "unprocessed" corpses; a medium-sized mound of "processed" male corpses that are naked and stacked orderly; and a covered, processed mound of women and children.

Though they are present in the larger mound, no female corpses are ever seen. This is a dramaturgical and ethical choice. This means Lavinia, Tamora, and the Nurse are not seen. Dresses and jewelry are amongst the items pillaged from the mound of unprocessed bodies, but when we see these items they are not on the bodies of the dead (they are either worn by Janice, put on the male bodies by Gary, or free from bodies).

PROLOGUE

A lush curtain hides the world behind.

Carol enters. She receives entrance applause and isn't sure what's happening. Perhaps they're applauding because her throat is slit, which it is. She holds it with one hand so she won't bleed out.

CAROL

Like God, a sequel hides inside an ending:
When time is up you pray that it's extending.
For life, to cultured, and to the philistine
Once felt, is craved 'til thrills become routine.
But once routine the thrills, to thrill, must grow.
And if they don't, an outrage starts to show.
So double up on savagery and war:
To satisfy you multiply the gore.

(Blood squirts from her throat. The squirt has a big arch.)

> You make the aftermath a catapult
> To pageantries of battle. The result:
> A feasting on the gore 'til you are ill;

(More blood squirts.)

> Until you vomit what did once fulfill.
> To feast we start inside a banquet room,
> But one whose table is a bloody tomb.
> A scene so monstrous it sends up the savage,

(Blood squirts from both sides of her neck.)

> Presumably to snuff what makes us ravage.
> But making spectacle of vengeance, do we pause?
> Or spur it on with centuries of applause?
> In grappling, here and now, with all that's past
> We wonder how to slow what's been too fast?

(She takes her hand away from the wound. Blood runs down her for the rest of the Prologue. What was funny is now disturbing.)

> Will we surpass the past or be its equal?
> Will we affirm or break the bloody sequel?
> Intensify 'til cruelty does cascade?
> Or let the cleanup come? Enter the maid.

(Carol looks stage left as Gary enters, pulling a mop and bucket with him. We hear entrance applause. Gary, who doesn't notice Carol, looks into the audience.)

GARY
A maid just enters and he gets applause?
Best first day on the job that ever was.

(Climactic symphonic music plays. Carol grabs the curtain's rope for support, then passes out, pulling the curtain open and disappearing amongst it [or she grabs the curtain and pulls the entire thing down with her, disappearing underneath it].

We are in Titus Andronicus's opulent banquet room, during the Roman Empire and a few hours after the coup, which transpired at the end of Shakespeare's Titus Andronicus. Nothing has been cleaned. Instead, the banquet room has been used as a storage space for the aftermath. There are at least one thousand male corpses onstage. Stage right, encroaching into the center, is chaos. Bodies are everywhere, including a dump-heap mound of them, which one may climb, that reaches at least fourteen feet high. There's a smaller covered mound of bodies as well [where the women and children are kept and unseen throughout].

The stage left side of the room has been set up as a workstation: various instruments, buckets, and accoutrements needed for the task of cleaning/organizing corpses.

The music comes to a climactic finish.)

SCENE 1

GARY

Bit more of them than I was expecting.

(Slight pause.)

Sorta difficult to know where to begin.

(Slight pause.)

Me mum always said, "When cleaning, Gary, ya start at the top and work your way down."

(Slight pause.)

Alright then.

(Gary steps into the large mound of bodies and begins to climb. To the dead:)

Sorry. Oh. Sorry about that. I'll just put my foot there and—
Right. Don't mind me. Sorry about the face. Oh. Slippery one.

(While climbing:)

Two boys in here got baked inside two pies.
Long story short, most everybody dies.
(Bragging:)
I had a part in it,
(A confession:)
A little brief.
I guess I'm what you'd call, comic relief.
A joke, that's what I was, and not a good one.
'Cause when that joke's on you, it ain't that fun.
I used to juggle pigeons in the gutter.
So didn't clean but helped to make the clutter:
I always was a clown who hated clowns.
Ya know the type who stumbles 'bout the towns
With off-timed jokes invariably that flop,
And so becomes a target for the slop—
For when your talent's barely juggling birds
It makes a bloke a bull's-eye for the turds—
Not metaphorical and not from fowl
But actual poo found in a human bowel.
My great-great-granddad was a clown. They claim
He wasn't good as well but all the same
He passed routines on down to us that followed
And every generation grinned and swallowed
Our place inside the square with poo and pigeons
As clowning was inherited like religions.
I never had the reins of me own doing
Me choices were what others were pursuing.

Like that there Titus general before me,
His tale when told did use then did ignore me.
It was the same old same, rich folk want power,
Revenge, and center stage, and will devour
The little folk like me along the way.
So yeah, they killed some folk in this buf*fet*,
They speechified and then they had a sob,
But all you need to know's: I got a job.
Yeah really that is it, no need to stress
Or even read a little synop . . . sess.
I get it, some will wish they'd done their study
But either way all this would still be bloody.
So let me say it clear, all that ya need:
That Titus bloke is dead; now I'm the lead.
For this here works an opportunity.
They'll be no begging for the coin for me.
They'll be no eggs, insults, or poo I'll dodge,
Not with this job, me foot's inside the lodge.
Me foot's inside the court! Next comes the rest!
Me clowning days are done, I got a quest
To raise me status, climb up top the ladder.
So watch this cameo begin to matter!

(Gary suddenly sinks in the mound until we can't see him.)

SCENE 2

The servants' door opens. We hear screams and battle sounds from outside.

Janice enters with a wheelbarrow of corpses, shouting off:

JANICE

OH DON'T MIND ME, I'LL GET THE DOOR MESELF.

(Entrance applause is heard. Aside to the audience, dismissing their applause:)

Yeah, yeah, yeah how 'bout a raise?

(Gary, opening a door, made from a corpse, and coming out of the bottom of the mound:)

GARY

Hello Janice, my name is—

JANICE

Gary! What ya doing here?

GARY

Now you're supposed to say, "Hello Gary, my name is Janice."

JANICE

What, is that some kind of routine?

GARY

Well gotta make a good impression on a first day of work.

JANICE

What ya on about?

GARY

I got a job.

JANICE

With me?

GARY

I know, isn't it fun? Best day ever.

JANICE

But you're the street clown.

GARY

Yeah, got a promotion.

JANICE

From clown to maid?

GARY

'Cause all the other maids got killed in the coup.

JANICE

So they sent me a clown as if anyone can do the cleaning?

GARY

I ain't no anyone.

JANICE

Ain't that just the way it is.

GARY

More like an everyman who's a nobody else.

(During the following they unload the wheelbarrow.)

JANICE

Well I ain't got time to debate it, so start unloading the dead. We gotta get this banquet room cleaned before the inauguration they're holding here in the morning—

GARY

Really?—

JANICE

In all these years I ain't never. I'm at me lowest. And the fingers are twitching on the swords, Gary, ready to stab a couple of maids dead for failing at a job. So stop your naysay and get a pep in your step already.

GARY

But the coup ain't even done yet and the new emp'ror's having an inauguration?

JANICE

Oh ya know the higher-ups, they like to say they've finished a job before actually doing it. And it's pronounced em-per-or.

GARY

Emp'ror?

JANICE

Em-per-or.

GARY

Emp'ror?

JANICE

Em-per-or.

GARY

Right, that's what I said: emp'ror.

JANICE

Em-per-or.

GARY

It's pronounced emp'ror?

JANICE

Em-per-or.

GARY

Right, that's what I said: emp'ror.

JANICE

Em-per-or.

GARY

It's pronounced emp'ror?

JANICE

Em-per-or.

GARY

Emp'ror?

JANICE

PER-OR! Why clowns always gotta speak in a cockney?

GARY

It's funny.

(Gary honks a hidden horn that he keeps in the armpit of his costume. He uses it to emphasize things.)

JANICE

You're a Roman.

GARY

What am I supposed to do, talk in the Latin?

JANICE

Ya gotta be a clown about everything?

GARY

Janice, ya ever wonder if the thing you're complaining about is the thing ya do yourself?

JANICE

Well I know I talk in a cockney. Sensible or not, it's me place as a maid. But when a clown does it, you're making me place a joke. I ain't a joke. Ya hear me?

GARY

It ain't a clown who gets themselves out of a hanging?

JANICE

What ya on about?

GARY

It all started when I did this favor for one so Mr. Titus.

JANICE

General Titus?

GARY

He stopped me on the street, in front of a whole bunch of his blokes, and told me to deliver a note to the emp'ror.

JANICE

I worked for that general his whole life, he never even once said hello to me.

GARY

Probably a good thing, as that note he gave *me* ended up having me knife in it.

JANICE

What you mean?

GARY

Yeah. And when the emp'ror saw the knife, he took that as a threat, and sent me off to be hanged.

JANICE

Why'd ya put your knife in the note?

GARY

I didn't do it. General Titus did.

JANICE

But ya delivered it?

GARY

Well it was exciting going to court and I forgot the knife was there.

JANICE

Ya can't feel something a bit inflexible in a piece of parchment?

GARY

Well it could have been a stick or something.

JANICE

Why'd someone send an em-per-or a stick?

GARY

I don't know, just doing what I was told and got caught up in a intrigue. *(A discovery in the moment)* Hey Janice, ya think that Titus chose me because he thought I didn't matter?

JANICE

General Titus. War-mongering-mass-murderer or not, gotta be respectful.

GARY

He wasn't respectful of me. Thought I was a silly fellow. Sorta a disposable. But I didn't get hanged, did I? Or stabbed dead like he did. 'Cause I figured out me maneuver.

JANICE

Don't be talking dirty.

GARY

But in the moment at the gallows pit
It's then me noggin had a little wit,
Janice.
"Gary this noose ain't gotta be your death;
They'll need a maid, now that most ain't got breath."
And right there then, once tasting a solution
The flavor spurred me on, past persecution.
So when they asked for my last words I said,
"I want a better job to earn me bread."

I took the reins of life, used common sense:
"You need a bloke to clean and to dispense
Of all the dead, well it would be a priv'lege,
And stop more mess from me own dangling dribb'lege."
And here's the point; it ain't fortuity.
That there was me first ingenuity.
And knock me over they agreed. They did.
"Go clean the banquet room, Sirrah," I kid
Ya not, as if the plan were theirs they'd made
And not the little clown's who got them swayed.
(Aside:)
And calling me Sirrah, all arbitrary
When everybody knows me name is—

JANICE

Gary, ya gonna talk like that all day?

GARY

What ya mean?

JANICE

Why ya rhyming?

GARY

Was I?

JANICE

I can't abide rhyming. Sorta irritating. Sorta like you're peck-
ing at me brain.

GARY

Never rhymed before. Ooo, me ingenuity is picking up the
speed.

JANICE

Well keep it to yourself and get to work.

GARY

Oh alright. So what I thought we'd do—

JANICE

What, ya want to be in charge?

GARY

Well they did sorta tell me—

JANICE

Oh they told ya did they?

GARY

Well it was assumed it was part of the bargain—

JANICE

It was assumed?

GARY

Am I not in charge?

JANICE

I want ya to look at me, in the face, and tell me what ya think the answer to that is.

GARY

But—

JANICE

In the face.

(Gary looks at her.)

GARY

(Worst day ever) OH NOOOOOO.

JANICE

What, ya saying ya'd rather be dead than have me in charge?

GARY

Might be?

JANICE

Gary—

GARY

But it was part of me consideration in taking the position—

JANICE

Ain't this the way it is. I spend me life in service, learning an expertise on how to right a room, and what does it get me? Does it give me respect? An assumption of a leadership position? Or do I instead get saddled with a rhyming clown who claims he should be in charge because it was part of his consideration?

GARY

I'm sorry Janice, it's just—

JANICE

YA THINK THIS IS ME FIRST MASSACRE? Ya think I sat around idle on the Ides of March? Ya think the mangled man-parts of Marcus Manlius just rolled themselves off the scene? Oh no. Someone had to collocate the duties, marshal the maids, assemble the scrubbers. And that someone was me. Time and time again. *(Aside)* I'm a lot older than I look. *(Back to Gary)* And ya think today's coup was self-contained in this little bit of dining room? Just a couple a blokes baked in a pie, a couple more stabbed through? Ya think the streets are all clean and nifty? Ya know as well as I it's a hell on earth out there and only getting worse, what with the autocracy turned to a democracy turning back to an autocracy as we speak. But who ya think is gonna get it sorted? Who ya think got the bright idea of taking a space like this, already sullied by a slaughter, and turning it into a holding room, a sorta storage space, for the rest of the slaughter? Ya think that was the idea of some pigeon-juggler? Oh no, that would have to come from someone who's been at it before. Someone who understands ya put the murder and the mayhem in one place to make it easier to see what's what!

GARY

But—

JANICE

Now you listen to me! I got ten more years before I can put up me plates, and me aches and pains are traveling faster than the years. And that means I got me own considerations to consider. And my considerations have to do with me telling you what work to do and you DOING IT!

GARY

But it's not about getting the job done.

JANICE

What's that supposed to mean?

GARY

Well, and it's just a theory, but a scene like this might indicate that the coup people took over the empire because . . . they were a little mad at it.

JANICE

(Snark) Ya think?

GARY

So if a sabotage is what they had in mind, I figure we do as little as possible, try to have some fun, and maybe we'll get promoted.

JANICE

That's what you figure?

GARY

I'm ingenious now. So you understand why I gotta be in charge.

JANICE

Well, perhaps if I didn't need to prove meself with the new leadership to keep me livelihood and life, or if the literal rigor mortis setting in here, as well as the metaphorical one out there, weren't fast approaching and about to make the job of cleaning an impossibility, or perhaps if the world weren't in TOTAL COLLAPSE RIGHT NOW, or even if you'd actually done something when I'd come in, I might be interested in your . . . ingenuity. But as it is, you're just plopping about.

GARY

Oh now—

JANICE

So it don't matter if them people out there put ya in charge. All that matters is what these people— *(Gesturing to the two of them)* in here think. And as one of these people, ya might want to accept the leadership of someone who knows a thing or two. Ya might want to be better than them clowns out there and respect a little AUTHORITY OF SUBJECT.

GARY

(Bursting into tears) Ahhhhhhh.

JANICE

What ya crying for?

GARY

The state of the world.

SCENE 3

JANICE

(While hauling a corpse onto her workstation and then taking its weapon off of it) Well there ain't no use in sobbing. So first things first we gotta separate the accessories, weapons, and people.

GARY

(Recovered from crying) Really?

JANICE

In death as in life. So ya put the men in the heap and the women and children under here.

GARY

How come ya covered them?

JANICE

I don't like looking at dead women and children, is that alright with you? Next ya gotta strip the torsos.

(In one fast move she strips the entire corpse naked.)

Then, ya jiggle them about to set free any excess gas they got.

(Janice picks up and shakes the naked corpse. There's lots of flatulence. Speaking over the flatulence:)

Ya might think you're done with it at a certain point but people always got more than ya want them to have.

(She shakes the body and the last remains of flatulence seep out.)

Next ya make a small cut above the navel. That's where ya insert this tube into the abdomen and pump out the contents of the intestines.

(Black goo pumps out of the body, spraying into a bucket.)

It takes about twenty to thirty pumps.

(She does this for a good twenty to thirty pumps before talking again.)

Then ya make a cut in a main artery. *(Aside)* I prefer the armpit to the groin as it seems less invasive. *(To Gary)* Ya gotta siphon out all the blood, so get a good suction. Be certain ya use this tube for the feces and this one for the blood, otherwise when you're sucking, ya might get a face of fluid ya don't want. Ya know what I mean?

(Janice sucks on the tube until the blood starts flowing into a different bucket.

Pause.)

GARY

Janice . . . ya ever think ya don't want to do the job you've been assigned?

JANICE

No point in that.

GARY

Just seems, if this is the kind of thing ya gotta do on the regular, ya might not be living your best life.

JANICE

What ya think I got a choice? The options just opened up to any who want them?

GARY

Just seems some folk get to do the fun jobs and other folk gotta do the . . . not-fun jobs.

JANICE

Way of the world, so get to it.

(They work. Gary tries to do everything right but fails. He can't help himself. He's a clown. He strips a torso in such an awkward way the outfit ends up on him. He gets distracted by the flatulence and makes musical compositions.

He pumps out the goo and gets the dry heaves, which turns his movement into an odd modern dance routine. He siphons the blood but loses his grip and blood sprays all over.

Janice, who is doing everything right, is too focused on her work to notice.)

SCENE 4

GARY

Sorta not the best day ever anymore. *(Seeing a handsome corpse; an aside)* Ooof, that's a handsome-looking bloke. *(To Janice)* Hey Janice. Janice.

JANICE

What?

GARY

This one got a leading-man physique.

JANICE

Gary!

GARY

Just saying, he's the sorta bloke when passing him on the street, you turn around to see the backside of. Ya know what I mean?

JANICE

What, ya saying you're attracted to that there corpse?

GARY

Well . . . he got a bit of a noncommittal charm. Kind of bloke who draws you in by not giving much.

JANICE

You put him down and work on that one over there.

GARY

Oh alright.

(Gary works on a less attractive corpse but still manages to find a way to like him. He starts puppeteering the corpse.
Janice works.)

Janice?

JANICE

What?

GARY

"Look, I'm a corpse."

JANICE

Stop that!

GARY

Just Fooling.

JANICE

Just running around acting disrespectful.

GARY

Well *you* put the men in the open.

                    JANICE
What ya mean?

                    GARY
Ya didn't cover them like the women and children.

                    JANICE
That's different.

                    GARY
Is it?

                    JANICE
Being that we've never had a female emperor, one might con-
clude the men are a little more responsible for a thing like this.
So forgive me if I don't treat the blokes with me total sensitiv-
ity. Don't mean ya can be using them as your playthings the
way they use the women. Over and over, since them Persians
kidnapped Io making the Greeks kidnap Medea and Europa,
making the Persians kidnap Helen, because everybody wanted
two captured princesses to make it even. But two wasn't
enough, so the entire history of conflict is a bunch of men shuffling princesses. And who ya think had to clean the mess. All
the way from the Sabines, Lucretia, Agnes, and now Lavinia.

(Janice suddenly bursts into tears.)

                    GARY
Sorta over-the-top what happened to Lavinia.

                    JANICE
Scrubbed up after that Titus girl her whole life. Little finger-
prints on the banister.

                    GARY
Oh, cry it out. I bet that feels good.

JANICE

Stop that. Bad clown. The only thing I can do to help her now is put this scene to rest. So get to work.

(They work in silence.)

I mean really.

(They work in silence.)

Treating the dead that way.

(They work in silence and continue working during the following:)

You're a maid now. That means ya can't be making a spectacle of yourself, bringing attention. "Oh my name is Gary." How ya think I survived when none of the other maids did? I'm the best there is and nobody remembers me name. That's how! And I ain't about to be remembered by association, so keep ya head down, do the work, and stop your Fooling.

GARY

Ya ever seen a Fool?

JANICE

Is that a trick question?

GARY

Not a fool. A Fool, like a clown, but a step up. A clown with ambition.

JANICE

What, them clowns in the court that insult people?

GARY

Them's ain't clowns, them's Fools.

JANICE

Jokesters all the same to me.

GARY

(The most horrible thing he's ever heard) Oh! Janice! That's—
Oh! Now that's just— Oh! How— . . . CLOWNS AND
FOOLS IS TOTALLY DIFFERENT!

JANICE

(Meaning "whatever") Hmmhmmm.

GARY

The clown encourages the idiotic
By getting laughs and praise for being dumb.

*(Gary jiggles the gas out of a corpse to show a clown being
dumb.)*

But Fools, they tease out our stupidity
With brains, so spark our feelings and our smarts.

JANICE

If ya say so.

GARY

The clown's a selfish bloke whose only goal's
To satisfy his belly, heart, and groin.
But Fools are empathetic sorts who learn
The suffering of others 'cause they've been
Thrown out of homes and had the poo of life
Thrown at them just for being different-from.
And so while clowns are in it for themselves,
A FOOL'S AMBITION IS TO SAVE THE WORLD!

Ya know what I mean?

JANICE

No. Ya confused me by talking in the verse without the rhyme.
Don't know whether me brain's getting pecked at or not.

GARY

(A discovery) I'm changing me ways. Using me ingenuity.
Janice?

JANICE

What?

GARY

I'm gonna tell ya a secret.

JANICE

Oh dear.

GARY

I ain't never told nobody. Not even meself.

JANICE

Well don't start.

GARY

But it's the day for it. The coup made a crack. Ya gotta let
things out when there's a crack—

JANICE

You're making me uncomfortable.

GARY

I don't think I can stop. It's crawling up me.

JANICE

Well squash it down.

GARY

It's bubbling out me groin.

JANICE

That's not a good thing.

GARY

It's reached me heart.

JANICE

Well hold your breath and swallow.

GARY

I WANT TO BE A FOOL.

JANICE

(Meaning, sarcastically, "You've succeeded") Congratulations.

GARY

But this could have been me today! That's a near-death experience I had.

JANICE

Every day for every person is a near-death. It's called life. It ain't a badge of honor.

GARY

But a person who is stuck in an intrigue, ya telling me that ain't special?

JANICE

That's what's called a casualty.

GARY

A casualty ain't special?

JANICE

No, 'cause it's too casual.

GARY

Seems the casualty is how casual it is.

JANICE

Boohoo, we're the dregs of Romulus.

(During the following, Gary works.)

GARY

Sorta numbing that. Accepting a lot in life. Stuck in a routine. In our own sorta sequel. But ooo boy saving meself today, bit surprising. Sorta gave me a feeling. The only thing that makes a feeling really. Doing a thing that's surprising. And feeling it. Well, that catapulted me into other things that are surprising. Ya know Janice, on me way here, I noticed the sky. I hadn't ever really noticed the sky before. Sure I'd seen it lots. And heard people talk about how pretty a sunset is. But I always feel, when people ooo and ahh over a thing that happens every day, as if it were some grand surprise, I want to say something cheeky during the sunset like, "Guess what? It goes down."

JANICE

That's not nice.

GARY

Yeah. I suppose I'm the sorta person who likes to ruin other people's performance of a feeling. But here I was surprised by my surprise over how the sky was actually sorta pretty. Don't get me wrong, I wasn't surprised by the prettiness of the sky but more the surprise of my surprise that the sky was pretty, ya know what I mean? Gave me a pep in me step, that did. To me first day of me new job. But then, watching you pump out them intestines, sorta had another feeling. And I thought, Well Gary, maybe you should encourage them to hang ya again, so ya can feel that more better feeling ya had from getting yourself out of the hanging. But that would be a repeat, wouldn't it? That would be a sequel and not something new and so not surprising. Yeah, that would be more a performance of surprise. I wasn't after a repeat. I was after that feeling of a feeling. 'Cause once ya feel that, it's proof ain't it? Proof ya don't gotta live your life accepting the muck. And what's that mean? Others don't either. Oh Janice, I can't be cleaning this.

(Gary throws down whatever instruments he's been cleaning with.)

I GOT A RESPONSIBILITY!

JANICE

What, to get us killed?

GARY

(Excited) Gotta save the world. Gotta make, not just meself better, but . . . all sorts of things. And now that I got a job in a fancy place, I could find me way to the court, couldn't I? Become one of them blokes who changes the minds of emp'rors. Someone who gets a promotion from clown, to maid, to Fool!

JANICE

What, being a maid ain't enough?

GARY

No, just—

JANICE

No I understand. Ya ain't got respect for them that gotta do the dirty work and instead ya want to flop about insulting people?

GARY

No, that's just one of the perks.

JANICE

Gary! Ya ain't got enough smarts to even be a good clown. Oh but here ya are expecting to save the world? I mean ya can't even choose the proper juggling equipment.

GARY

Can too.

JANICE

Then why pigeons instead of a few simple balls?

GARY

Well ya gotta love a pigeon.

JANICE

Ya ever wonder why when ya throw them up, they never come down?

GARY

That's sorta the joke. You're missing it.

JANICE

No I think *you're* missing the joke. 'Cause the joke is you. Oh is that surprising? Did that give ya a feeling? Well how's this for a feeling. You're common. No, you're worse than common. You're a commoner smelling like shit with an agenda to spread it around. *(Mocking)* "Oh, I can save the world." No. What ya can save is the first obstacle in front of ya. Me floor. And you've gotten me behind schedule, so juggle your ambition of foolery the same way ya do with your birds—

(Janice mimes juggling birds and having them fly away.)

Ya crying again?

GARY

(He is) No.

JANICE

(Pointing to a spot on the floor) What's that?

GARY

I don't know.

JANICE

I think that's a teardrop coming out a weak little clown.

GARY

I'm sorry Janice.

JANICE

Wipe it up.

GARY

The first obstacle in front of ya?

JANICE

That's right.

(Janice sucks. Gary mops.)

GARY

(Aside:)

An obstacle could be a wall like rock;
Or be a person always out to block.
Who never has a laugh because they're stuck
Regurgitating other people's muck.

(Janice pulls some entrails out of a body.
Aside:)

Who will humiliate those who rebel
Because their change will force her to as well.
But every wall, especially those that think,
Is vulnerable for has itself a chink.
And what's in front of me that is Tyrannus,
Me obstacle to save, is clearly Janice.

I don't think ya mean to be mean Janice.

JANICE

Oh no, I do.

GARY

But look at ya. Having an unseen role in the scheme of things.
Never being noticed or respected. To the point where ya don't
even know what a pleasure is anymore.

JANICE

What, I don't know how to have a frolic? A pint at the pub?
Wearing me best?

GARY

No just, I never seen ya dressed up.

JANICE

I ain't saying I done it. Ya think me pay gets a closet of fancy?

GARY

Oh look! Got the fancy right here!

(Gary picks up a necklace.)

JANICE

You put that down.

GARY

Nobody will see.

JANICE

We ain't being a cliché to our class.

GARY

Well I'd sure work faster with a little pep in me step from a surprise from seeing you wearing a bauble.

JANICE

What ya mean?

GARY

Sorta need something pretty to look at to get ya doing the ugly work. And I bet it'd look pretty on you.

JANICE

Oh Gary—

GARY

Ya gotta inspire people to action.

                              JANICE
Ya saying I put on this bauble, you'll double your work and
get us back on schedule?

                               GARY
Ain't nothing put a pep in a step like a surprise from a sparkle.

(Slight pause.)

                              JANICE
Give it here.

(Janice puts on the necklace.)

Now get that pep in your— *(Seeing the bauble on herself)* Oh
that is nice isn't it? Oh. Bit unexpected. That . . . feeling.

                               GARY
The one where ya didn't wake thinking you'd be looking like
a respectable?

                              JANICE
Don't be blabbing your mouth about it.

                               GARY
Of course, me lady.

                              JANICE
Oh Gary.

                               GARY
(Putting a cape on her) Your cape, me lady.

                              JANICE
(Acting upper class) Oh yes. Oh my. Oh what to do to do to
do?

GARY

Shall we go on a-hunting?

JANICE

I do like a rummage.

GARY

(Making a horn noise) Doo doo doo doooooooo.

JANICE

(A charge) Yaaaaa!

(Hunting music rings out. They dive, disappearing into a heap of dead.)

GARY

(Unseen) All sorts of jewels and rings and shiny things down here.

(Appearing) Oooo, I found a ding-dong bracelet.

(Appearing, wearing a mismatch of fancy) Ya know you're someone when ya got enough to bejewel your privates.

(Suddenly seeing Saturninus) Bloody hell, there's me dead emp'ror. *(To Saturninus)* Bet ya didn't think it'd turn out like this. Me standing over ya. Still you're looking great. There are three stages of life ya know: youth, middle age, and, "You're looking great."

(Picking up two severed hands and making them clap for him and performing as if in a comedy club) Oh thanks, great to be back at the house of Titus Andronicus.

(Dropping the hands) Saturninus. Funny name that. Naming your baby after a planet. Sorta ambitious right from the get-go? Not so ambitious now. Still sorta fancy with the crown. Funny they didn't take it with them.

(Takes the crown off Saturninus)

Oooo. Not fancy now.

(Puts it back on)
Fancy again. Sorta all it took, isn't it?
(Takes it off)
Oooo, not fancy.
(Puts it on)
Fancy.

(Gary pulls the crown off Saturninus's head, and the entire head detaches from the body with it.)

Ahhhhh.

(Gary throws the head away and keeps the crown. To the crown:)

What we do with you now? *(Putting the crown on)* Fancy!

(Entrance music for Janice. She enters from the middle of the mound by moving a corpse. It moves like a door. She is all vamped out, wearing a completely different outfit. Her hair has been done up in an over-the-top glamorous style.)

JANICE

How do I look?

GARY

Rule the banquet hall, Janice.

JANICE

Friends, Romans, Countrymen.

GARY

Oh speech it.

JANICE

Aw no, sorta garish. Loading yourself down with the bauble. *(Taking off a bauble)* I mean look at me, so much ya can barely see any skin. *(To an audience member)* What you looking? Oh, you want a little more. Oh, what's happening? Oh, a little bauble on. A little bauble off.

(Janice throws baubles into the audience.)

GARY

Oh spread the wealth.

JANICE

(Throwing baubles) You want a bauble. Here's a bauble for ya. *(Still taking off baubles in a burlesque)* I mean we got plumbing. If we can move something as complicated as our waste and water, it shouldn't be too difficult to spread a little wealth. And while we're at it, some shelter would be nice. Oh and a meal. *(Becoming a galvanizing speech)* Couldn't be too hard to feed the people instead of trying to look like a walking constellation. Yeah, we're the ones that make the ways to run the world. So we're the ones who must invent the ways to rise until the last is first and first is last. 'Til then, the righteous give a bauble up.

GARY

Oh Janice, you're missing a piece.

(Gary puts the crown on her head.)

JANICE

What'd you just put on me head? Oh that's—that's—

GARY

The gold laurel.

JANICE

Ya trying to get me killed?

GARY

No, I'm having a—

JANICE

It's all tangled.

GARY

Oh Janice I'm having a—

JANICE

Gary, I got the empire stuck on me head.

GARY

I'm having a . . .

JANICE

Get it off.

GARY

I'm having a—

JANICE

What!?!

GARY

AN EPIPHANY!

JANICE

Well that's just indecent.

GARY

I know, that's an ingenuity, a responsibility, and an epiphany all in one day.

JANICE

What kind of degenerate are ya?

GARY

The kind standing here listening to you speechify and thinking, you should be the emp'ror. Oh, then I could be your Fool
and insult ya in the court. Wouldn't that be fun?

JANICE

Ya trying to make a joke of me?

GARY

Of course.

JANICE

So everyone would laugh at the maid wearing the crown.

GARY

Well they wouldn't laugh if ya won it.

JANICE

Oh ya think a maid can campaign to rule the empire? Get it
off.

GARY

Why not? It's a democracy. Sorta.

JANICE

No. Bit late for that. Maybe ya noticed, the only thing that
changes the leadership is making a spectacle. So unless ya
want to create a spectacle that's even bigger than all this, ain't
no one gonna pay attention to a maid.

GARY

(A lightbulb) Uh.

JANICE

And we got the inauguration banquet happening in the
morning.

GARY

All the court will be here to witness?

JANICE

And hang us both if we ain't finished.

GARY

But that's an opportunity. Standing at a noose. That's the moment ya get to be noticed. Even a maid. Oh the pieces are connecting. The inauguration. Me epiphany. The crown. You. A spectacle. It's turning into . . . it's turning into, it's—

JANICE

Stop your turning and help me clean the coup.

SCENE 5

GARY

THAT'S IT. WE'RE GONNA STAGE A COUP!

JANICE

Lower your voice!

GARY

The first is gonna be last.

JANICE

You're gonna get me hanged.

GARY

No you're gonna be the leader.

JANICE

Don't be saying that, even joking.

GARY

I'm not joking. I mean the coup's a joke but I'm not joking about it, ya know what I mean?

JANICE

No.

GARY

We're gonna make a spectacle that is its own kind of coup.

JANICE

We ain't got coup enough?

GARY

Not a violent coup. An artistic one. A sort of theatrical revenge on the Andronicus revenge. A comedy revenge to end all revenge. Well not just a comedy. A sorta folly. No a spectacle. Or a comedy folly that is a spectacle. Sorta a machination. That's full of laughter. But more than laughs. But with the laughs. Well sorta a thinking man's laughter. But could be a knee-slapper. So is a . . . or inspires a . . . or—

JANICE

Pick one and commit!

GARY

I don't know, but I know it's gotta have all the history in it. All the conflicts. Like you said, put all the murder and mayhem in one place so they can see what's what. What they've been. What they could be. Which means we gotta squeeze all the sequels of revenge in. We gotta theatricalize the sequels after the sequel after the sequels. And all the orgies of hyperbole, the grabbing of privacy and privates, takeovers, tantrums, endless campaigns, pillaged elections, apocalyptic-weather-spewing-forth-shark-attack-family-feuds! Yes Janice, shark attacks. There must be wars in stars, and geriatric stars at war. Heroes must battle heroes, winged rodents must clash with cleft chins, there must be an explosion of an explosion, a massacre of a massacre, an ensemble of an ensemble, to such a ridiculous degree ya can't see anything but its ridiculousness. And Janice, when the court sees it, they'll be a little taken aback at first. There'll be a moment of silence, don't kid yourself. But then, in the distance, one soul will feel a bubbling finding its way to their hands. "What am I doing?" they'll wonder. "Why am I clapping?" And they'll realize. They're clapping for hope. And soon it spreads. Not just one court member but two. Then more. Row after row, gaining speed, soon all the court, the clapping turns to cheering, then standing on their feet, on chairs, reaching ever higher to touch the ingenuity that could be theirs as well. If two maids could turn the hopelessness of a massacre into a coup of beauty, they too can imagine a better world. New ways of government will spring forth, new mechanisms of distribution. They'll strip their baubles, they'll be running naked through the banquet room, laying themselves prostrate to servants, making love to enemies and outsiders, bleeding their hearts, flooding through the streets, until the entire world is saved by . . .

(Gary pulls a pigeon out of his bag and throws it into the air. It disappears.)

WONDER!

JANICE
(A discovery, to herself) I'm dealing with a mental.

GARY
Well if a person hanging out in this ain't, something's wrong. But no more. We're bringing an end to tragedy.

JANICE

Ya think ya can bring an end to tragedy?

(Gary moves the penis of one of Janice's corpses so it's facing left when it was facing right.)

GARY

I just did.

JANICE

Gary!

GARY

Sorta on the small scale but—

JANICE

I'll have none of that! Ya gotta be bigger!

GARY

Right. What if we moved all the men's penises from right to left at the same time? Would that be enough to end all tragedy? Oh Janice, the corpses. We gotta use the corpses. *(An idea)* Quick! Help me tie this bloke and then hoist his body into the air.

JANICE

Stop that.

GARY

It's for the Fooling. Oh! That's it. It's a Fooling. We're making a Fooling. *(Aside, a brag)* I just invented a genre. You're welcome.

JANICE

Gary calm down—

GARY

Ain't no time for calm now.

(During the following, Gary runs around setting up his Fooling: tying intestines to arms of corpses [making them marionettes]; setting up corpses so they'll domino and create a ricochet of activities; he creates pulley systems, catapults, and reveals out of body parts. Janice is too dumbfounded to do anything for now. The actor, designers, and director should invent more specifics of this spectacle than are written [but no additional dialogue].)

JANICE

Where ya gonna get a shark? Or a cleft chin and a winged rodent?

GARY

I haven't worked that part out yet.

JANICE

Where ya gonna get an ensemble of an ensemble?

GARY

Well ya gotta help?

JANICE

(Managing Gary's crazy) Alright, so how 'bout we sort through this mound here, get it all clean, and then we'll be able to see which one of the dead has the type of chin you're looking for?

GARY

(Suddenly remembering) Me leading man. Oh he ain't got a cleft chin but he could be one of our heroes.

JANICE

I thought ya wanted to be more than a clown.

GARY

I'm not a clown. I'm a maid. About to get promoted to Fool. *(Handing Janice an intestine and a severed leg)* Here, tie this off at an angle.

JANICE

(Doing it) Don't you boss me.

GARY

I got vision now. Which is more than I can say about some people who only got the vision they've already seen.

(Gary disappears into the mound.)

JANICE

Is that what I am? Someone without the grand vision of you, oh mighty Fool. *(Realizing she's been doing his bidding)* What am I doing? *(Noticing Gary under the covered mound)* You leave them women be. Ya hear me?

(Gary comes out, carrying branches.)

GARY

Ooo look we can use these branches for a wedding canopy.

JANICE

PUT THOSE DOWN!

GARY

Bit of an overreaction.

JANICE

Them's Lavinia's.

GARY

What? She collected branches?

JANICE

She used them for arms when they chomped them off her.

GARY

Really?

JANICE

After raping her and cutting out her tongue. Being more cruel to her than anyone in the world for the entertainment of it. For the ridiculousness. For someone's Fooling.

GARY

Janice, you're scaring me.

JANICE

(Grabbing Gary and choking him almost to death) Yeah they want an entertainment. So what we do. We chop 'em up and put 'em in a pie. How's that for an entertainment. Not funny enough. No? And how about this? How 'bout a maid strangles herself a disrespecting clown? Makes herself one more corpse to clean. Is that funny enough for ya? Isn't it all just a good laugh?

(Carol suddenly emerges from the mound right next to where Gary is being strangled.)

CAROL

(An inhale of breath) Uhhhhh!

(A slight pause.)

Did someone say pie?

SCENE 6

Janice screams. Carol screams. Janice and Carol scream. Gary screams.

    Gary and Janice run around trying to escape each other but end up slipping and sliding on dead bodies. Blood sprays. They scream. The scream starts to calm until they're all breathing heavy.

JANICE

Carol?

CAROL

Hello.

GARY

Who's Carol?

JANICE

The midwife.

CAROL

My real name's Cornelia but everyone gets me confused with a more popular Cornelia so they call me Carol.

GARY

(Thinking it's a sign from the gods) A midwife just came out of a mound of dead to help birth a Fooling!

JANICE

Or her wound coagulated so she didn't bleed through.

GARY

(To Janice) Why ya gotta ruin the magic? *(To Carol)* We ain't gonna listen to her. She just tried to kill me.

JANICE

(Surprised) Sorta satisfying getting a frustration out.

GARY

(To Janice) That's two near-deaths in one day. Ya telling me that ain't special?

JANICE

(About to strangle him again) Well how 'bout we make it three then?

CAROL

Oh don't mind me. Fight about. I'm used to being ignored. Stuck in the middle like I am. Not rich. Not poor. They don't even have a word for my class. Just sort of middle . . . class. *(Realization)* I just invented a class.

GARY

I invented a genre.

CAROL

I got my throat slit by Aaron the Moor so no one would know he got the empress pregnant.

GARY

You win.

CAROL

Small part in the grand scheme of things.

GARY

Like me Carol—

CAROL

But not even seen. And not something to get worked up about if you can't remember. Not someone to get so angry over you'd slit their throat. All I did was deliver a black baby. What'd they think, it'd be white? That they could pass it off? No, it was too late. The empress had been having an affair with Aaron the Moor and now they wanted to kill the proof. But it was the empress that wanted the baby dead. And then the nurse too but I didn't want the baby dead. Just didn't want some foreign little one inheriting the empire. That's understandable. You have to protect your own to help yourself don't you? Especially when you're not even seen. Stuck in the middle. Supplicating morals to be noticed. Day after day until you find you aren't even willing to save a baby. Simply to be seen? Though the baby's father sees you. He knows you just stood by while people tried to kill his little one.

(As if Aaron is approaching her) Oh no, Aaron, don't, it's not my fault. Have mercy. Don't slit my throat. I SHOULD HAVE SAVED THE BABY!

(Acting like her throat has been slit) Urgha ga ga urgha ga ga urghhhhh. Thrown aside. Stumble stumble. Blood squirt. Stumble stumble. Look for help. Look for help. Getting weak. Dizzy. Hallucinate. People in the dark. Try to tell them. Stop the cycle. Feel faint. Blood squirts. A curtain. A maid. Applause. Hold on. Get dizzy. Falling. Darkness. Nothing but darkness. And the dead. All around. Hear voices. Something 'bout Fooling. Cleaning. Fooling. Screaming. Something about pie. Feel hungry. Wake up. Blood. Horror. Here. Now. IN THE ETERNAL DAMNATION OF HEEEEEEEELLLLLLL.

(Pause.)

JANICE

Should we have a spot of tea?

CAROL

I could use some clotted cream.

JANICE

Alright then, rummage around for a bit to eat, while Gary and I set up the table.

GARY

What about the Fooling? What about you just trying to kill me? What about the time pressure?

JANICE

THERE'S ALWAYS TIME FOR TEA! Plus we got three workers now, what with Carol showing up. Puts us back on schedule even with a little break.

GARY

But—

(During the following song they set up tea. Things are under and behind bodies so there is much activity and the tea setup is ridiculously elaborate [as if they are having tea for twenty]. The song begins a cappella but soon they are all making a three-person marching band, like percussive accompaniment, by banging on the various tea-setting items, the table, and corpses.)

JANICE

(Singing:)

> Well the tea time
> Is you and me time
> So it's the right time
> To be happy.

CAROL

Oh, I know this one.

JANICE AND CAROL

(Singing:)

> Yes in the tea time
> We'll agree time
> Is the best time
> To be gay.

JANICE

Come on Gary.

JANICE, CAROL AND GARY

(Gary not so sure but then getting into it:)

> For the rest of
> All the day time
> Might be hard
> Or might be blue

But when the—
Bells chime
That it's tea time
That's the glee time
For me and you.

                    JANICE

Pass the butter

               GARY AND CAROL

Ooo ooo

                    JANICE

Pass the cream

               GARY AND CAROL

Ooo ooo

                    JANICE

Pass the sweets sir

               GARY AND CAROL

Know what I mean?

                    JANICE

Pass the teacup

                    GARY

And you cheer up.

          JANICE, CAROL AND GARY

For the tea time is finally here.
Oh the tea time
Is you and me time
So it's the right time
To be happy

JANICE, CAROL AND GARY *(continued)*
Yes in the tea time
We'll agree time
Is the best time
To be gay.

CAROL

I found a whole pie barely sliced into.

JANICE

That'll do nice.

GARY

I don't think ya want to eat that.

JANICE

Ya think I don't know? *(To Carol)* Couple rapers got baked in that pie.

CAROL

Oh.

JANICE

I was standing in the back, not being noticed as usual, watching it happen. And there he was, Titus, in a chef's hat. And he plops that there pie down in front of that evil empress, and I'm thinking, Oh, she got her boys to rape me, Lavinia, and here she is gonna take a bite out of them. Well that'll be the ultimate revenge won't it? We'll be able to put it all to rest once she takes that bite. Feel a bit of closure knowing the baddies got their comeuppance. But no. There she is poised with her fork, about to carve into her savory, and what does Titus do? He tells that empress her boys are in the pie, before she eats them. So, of course she doesn't eat them does she? And sure Titus stabs her dead after he tells her. And then the

---

emperor kills Titus, the new emperor kills the old emperor. Blood spraying every which way. But all I'm thinking is, it's a missed opportunity. Not getting the satisfaction of seeing her munching away on her own children. Well alright. We'll finish the job. We'll clean the plate for her.

CAROL

I didn't want the baby killed.

JANICE

Yeah, we're on to pie now.

CAROL

Then why am I in Hell about to eat people?

JANICE

It's just the banquet room.

CAROL

Of Hell?

GARY

Sorta feels like Hell with the mad strangler.

JANICE

(To Carol) We turned it into a storage space. We're getting it all sorted.

CAROL

Like a judgment?

GARY

'Course we're Romans so do we believe in Hell or a big collection of dead people in the Underworld?

JANICE

(Trying to ignore Gary and offering a slice for Carol) How big a piece ya want luv?

CAROL

Not Hell?

GARY

'Course ever since the Christians came it's a bit of a pile on.

JANICE

(Regarding the pie-slice size) Ya gonna make me guess?

CAROL

I'm getting a judgment to decide if you're sending me to the Underworld AND Hell?

GARY

Bit of an escalation that.

JANICE

How 'bout three literal fingers worth?

GARY

All the horror over and over.

CAROL

(About what Gary's saying) Bigger and bigger.

JANICE

Oh alright bigger. That's the spirit.

(Janice slices an extremely large piece of pie for Carol.)

GARY

'Til a maid turns cannibal. But not surprising. Just an add-on.

JANICE

What, rapers in a pie ain't surprising?

GARY

Well it had happened before, in *The Metamorphoses*, when Procne fed her son to his rapist father.

CAROL

I should read more.

JANICE

But that was one person cooked and this was two.

(Janice plops the massive slice on a plate.)

CAROL

Do I have to?

JANICE

For me Lavinia.

CAROL

Bit of a racist.

JANICE

(Forgetting about tea) Lavinia?

CAROL

She liked to call black people "raven-colored."

JANICE

So it's alright she was violated, her hands and tongue cut off?

CAROL

Of course not. But it undercuts the empathy.

JANICE

Carol, the rules are ya gotta feel more empathy for the victim than the man who slit your throat.

GARY

So I don't gotta feel empathy for you then?

JANICE

What ya mean?

GARY

YOU WERE GONNA KILL ME!

JANICE

WELL YA DID DRIVE ME TO IT!

CAROL

Oh what does it matter, they kill ya anyway. I mean look at us, three disposables.

JANICE

What you mean three? I got a use.

GARY

Yeah, I'm gonna be a Fool.

JANICE

Ya don't get rid of someone who's the best at what they do.

CAROL

That's what *I* thought. *(A little snarky that Janice's job isn't as important as being a midwife)* But I guess delivering babies isn't as valuable as someone who sorts. It's just a matter of time. They'll kill you and then they'll laugh. And after, they'll send you here to storage, to confess the worst of you. *(Con-*

fessing the worst of her) I JUST STOOD THERE. I DIDN'T SAVE THE BABY. I DESERVE TO BE SENT TO THE UNDERWORLD HELL!

JANICE

I'm certain ya did all ya could.

GARY

Did she?

JANICE

Under the given circumstances.

CAROL

All the horror, over and over.

JANICE

And the baby's fine.

GARY

Is it?

JANICE

(To Carol) It's gonna be raised by the remaining Titus Family.

GARY

(Sarcastic) Well those are decent people.

JANICE

Well what was Titus supposed to do, be fine with someone destroying his daughter.

GARY

Well it ain't likely the baby will survive with a bunch of people making more slaughter, outside that door, while we're getting your closure.

CAROL

The baby's alive but NOW it'll die?

JANICE

Well there's not much we can do about it— *(Correcting the placement)* Oh! Forks go on the left.

GARY

There is something. You can be the emp'ror. We can make the Fooling and save the world.

CAROL

And the baby?

GARY

(To Carol) Sure, I'm bringing an end to tragedy.

CAROL

Can I help?

GARY

Ya can help with the shopping, I need a cleft chin, a shark—

CAROL

Oh.

GARY

Stay focused, Carol. A winged rodent—

CAROL

Like a pigeon?

GARY

Well that's insulting.

JANICE

Yeah a pigeon.

GARY

No, not a pigeon, a bat or a flying squirrel.

CAROL

Oh right.

JANICE

Where she gonna find a bat?

CAROL

(Looking under bodies on the tea table) There's bound to be one in the storage of Hell. Shopping as activism!

GARY

It's refreshing working with an optimist.

JANICE

(Shaming Gary) Shame on you. Taking advantage of someone suffering a traumatic state. *(Shoving the plate with the massive slice on it in front of Carol)* Here's your pie luv. *(To Gary)* Making her search for a thing she ain't gonna find.

CAROL

(Finding a dead rat underneath a corpse) I found one.

JANICE

That's a rat.

CAROL

(About to cry) Oh.

GARY

That's perfect. Just gotta glue some wings on it. *(To Janice)* Why ya gotta be literal? *(To Carol)* And when you're done with that I need an ensemble of an ensemble.

JANICE

That's my job.

GARY

Oh, ya want to do it now do ya?

JANICE

No—

GARY

Ya gonna help us change things or not?

JANICE

Ya think anyone can just rally up the masses?

GARY

Well ya did it before. Ya said: Collocate the duties, marshal the maids, assemble the scrubbers.

CAROL

I found a pheasant.

(Carol pulls the wings off the bird.)

JANICE

CAROL! WE ARE TRYING TO HAVE A TEA!

GARY

(Referring to the pie) We ain't gonna eat that. *(To Carol)* Ya ain't gotta eat that, Carol, animating yourself out of the dead like ya did. You're the sort who knows how to rise up.

CAROL

I am?

JANICE

No. You're the type who's smart enough to accept the world but clean her plate.

GARY

Ya don't gotta be tragic.

JANICE

Take a bite for the girls, Carol.

GARY

(To Carol) Don't let her squash ya down, like she does with herself.

JANICE

All them blokes crunching in your teeth.

GARY

That's how ya become a vengeful maid right there.

JANICE

Carol doesn't want to be judged poorly and be sent to the Underworld Hell does she?

CAROL

Oh no.

GARY

Carol knows that the only way out of the Underworld Hell is to help save the world.

JANICE

But Carol isn't gonna save the world because Carol is damaged—

CAROL

I prefer quirky—

GARY

Gary doesn't think Carol's damaged.

CAROL

You don't?

GARY

Gary thinks Carol's inspired.

JANICE

Carol ain't so gullible she'll be complimented into a lunacy.

CAROL

(Standing up for herself) CAROL THINKS SHE IS! In fact, Carol thinks she'd rather save the world than have you tell her her only option is to eat people! I'm not tragic. I'M COMEDIC!

(Carol throws the pie in her own face.)

(Pulling something out of her mouth) I found a cleft chin.

SCENE 7

GARY

I knew ya were magic.

CAROL

We're making a FOOLING!

JANICE

(Going a little crazy) Alright Janice, break's over. You're on your own. Ain't got your satisfaction, that's the way of the world, but ya do what ya can. Get back to the cleaning. Keep it together.

GARY

(Seeing something fun for the Fooling) Ooo, these two could have a headless sword fight.

CAROL

And I could glue wings on their heads and make cherubim.

JANICE

Might be an impossibility but ya go down with your integrity.

GARY

Ooo, and how 'bout we dress this bloke as a random shepherd girl, that'll be funny.

JANICE

When they go low, you go lower to scrub the floor. So first things first, strip the torsos. Then, ya jiggle them about.

CAROL

Oh what if we put one in a corner with a skull having an existential crisis?

JANICE

Next ya pump out the contents of the intestines.

CAROL

This day is so much better than when it started.

GARY

Isn't it?

CAROL

Actually being part of things.

JANICE

Use this tube for the feces and this one for the blood.

GARY

(Seeing the handsome bloke) Ooo, me handsome bloke.

                    JANICE
You put him down.

                    GARY
No, he's gonna be the groom in the wedding sequence.

                    JANICE
Look at him, he ain't a senator, a tribune, he's just a citizen
who got wrapped up in it all and he needs someone to treat
him right.

                    CAROL
I wouldn't mind treating him right.

                    JANICE
Oh so you're gonna use the dead for a laugh now too?

                    GARY
Ya can't bring it back to the way it was. Ya gotta make something with it. Ooo we could have the women do dance moves.

                    JANICE
I warned you about them!

                    CAROL
I am tired of seeing dead women in stories.

                    JANICE
Thank you Carol.

                    GARY
But wouldn't ya like to see a bunch of them all in a line kicking in the same direction?

                    CAROL
Still dead though.

GARY

It could symbolize a revolt from tragedy.

CAROL

Still in the storage of Hell.

JANICE

Just more plopping about.

GARY

Then maybe I could have the soldiers do it?

JANICE

Just more shuffling. Making a mess ya can confuse with a purpose. Plopping and shuffling. Revolt after revolt. Never thinking a revolt could be to clean.

GARY

CLEANING IS IMMORAL.

(Janice stops working.)

Dirt and disorder changed your life so now ya go about making it all nice and clean and great, again, even though it was never really nice and clean and great in the first place, because the massacre of it was always floating about, just under the surface, and all you've done is make it seem pleasant for the people making the mess, instead of doing the work of actually turning it into something good, because ya don't know how to live in a goodness, 'cause ya never have, and ya think the only thing moral is what ya know, even though ya don't know and could never know if ya don't know the good in life, well, when a person cleans like that, their mop is as unethical as a sword. You're the one shuffling, Janice. Shuffling girls, from playrooms to graves. So worried about taking care of the dead but not actually caring enough to do something about their dying.

JANICE

I understand. Ya had some near-deaths. It changed your lives. And now ya think ya can change other people's as well. But it don't work that way. When ya refuse to pick up a mess so people see the error of their ways, they don't see the error, they get accustomed to it. They start thinking it's normal, and when something is normal it's your identity and when it's your identity, anybody who tries making something different out of the normal thing is trying to make you different and when someone is trying to make you different ya feel ya need to defend yourself, so what do ya do?

CAROL

I scrunch up in a wee ball.

JANICE

Ya make an even bigger massacre! And then ya got the rats, disease, more dead, a smell wafting through the streets, then the home prices go down, people start fleeing the city, refugees, people fighting for cleaner land, causing more death, and so on until the entire world looks just like this room. So, yes, you're ingenious but unless ya want to be responsible for the fall of the Roman Empire, BEST GET CLEANING!

(Janice sucks the wrong tube.)

GARY

Oh Janice. I think ya sucked the wrong tube.

CAROL

I don't know what that means.

GARY

(To Carol) Oh look at her. She don't know what to do, does she? Sorta so awful she can't even take the tube out. After the poo would get flung at me, I'd get confused too. Should ya

make a scene? But then that draws more attention. Should ya grin and bear it? Sort of act like it didn't happen? *(To Janice)* Oh don't look like that. You're suppose to be the emp'ror. I demoted ya, didn't I? I got ya frustrated to the point of sucking the wrong tube. Oh Janice, I turned you into a CLOWN!

(Gary sobs. Carol cries with him.)

CAROL

I didn't try and stop them from killing the baby.

GARY

Carol, we're focusing on Janice now. *(To Janice)* We gotta get that tube out.

(Carol cries loudly. Janice shakes her head no.)

Come on, on the count of three. One.

(Gary pulls the tube out, ducks, and Janice projectile-vomits into Carol's face.)

CAROL

That is unpleasant.

GARY

Carol! Someone other than you is having a rough day.

CAROL

BUT I SHOULD HAVE SAVED THE BABY!

GARY

THEN DO IT! I tell ya what, ya are in the Judgment Place. 'Cause we're judging ya. But we got ya sorted now. And we're gonna give ya a second chance. Right through those doors. To the world of the living.

CAROL

Where I can save the baby?

(Janice pukes in a bucket.)

GARY

And I can help Janice.

CAROL

Through those doors?

GARY

(To Carol) That's right. *(To Janice)* That's it, get all the clown out of ya.

CAROL

But how could I do it if I'm not even seen?

GARY

Maybe because you're not seen!

CAROL

My feet won't move.

GARY

Sneak in and save the baby.

CAROL

But then the baby's seen but I'm not seen?

GARY

CAROL, STOP BEING SO MIDDLE CLASS AND SAVE THAT GODDAMN BABY!

CAROL

NOOOO—

(Janice pulls the curtain closed on Carol and Gary. All is silent.)

JANICE

I tried to reason, to set a good example.
I tried to listen and to be polite.
I tried impressing with me résumé,
I raised me voice, I scolded and was stern.
I tried deceit, coercion, bargaining,
I pleaded and I strangled him near death.
To show him what the danger is when one
Won't heel but mocks the wills of brutal men,
I even used a little bit of mime.
What's worse than that? What's lower than this low?
The only tool that's left, and so I'll rhyme.
(Slight pause)
How can one cope when chaos permeates
And if what makes some laugh, to you, just grates?
Or worse than grates, brings sorrow to the front.
Perhaps one simply sits to mull and punt?

Does anyone have a mint?

(If an audience member doesn't volunteer a mint, Janice says things like: "No really, I'm actually asking. Does anyone?" If they still don't offer one, she could say, "It's alright, I'll wait. Anyone?" If they still don't, she can ask sincerely, "Really?" If they still don't: She shrugs and continues on with the scene. If they do have one she can say, "Appreciate it." Or, if nobody in the orchestra has one and there's a balcony in the theater, "Feel free to throw one down from the balcony . . . I'll wait." If someone does, she can say, "Oh there ya go . . . you can just sort of pass that up to me . . . or . . . oh never mind . . . getting a little too elaborate." If she does get one and it's in a plastic wrapper or in a tin with paper around it, she unwraps the

mint as noisily as possible, while looking at an audience mem-
ber who, earlier, was unwrapping theirs. After a bit, Janice
picks up the branches that were left downstage of the curtain.)

> Lav'nia, when she was a little squirt,
> Would doctor trees, and flowers, beetles, dirt.
> She'd calmly wait for every heart to beat
> E'en if they ne'er had hearts. 'Twas her conceit
> That all things animate or not had souls.
> She'd bandage twigs, then mend half-eaten rolls.
> But as she grew, and lost so many brothers
> To wars from all our fear of all the others,
> Like most of us when hurt, she lost her play.
> Like maids who scrub the mess of hope away,
> Confusing it and dirt with the profane.
> So do not shift, or strive, but just maintain
> The way of life, the curse, revenge, the chase,
> How some will feel so much to feel no grace.
> The need for nothing to be felt, to cope.
> Then tasks become just like a hangman's rope,
> Ya pick things up to not see what you've dropped;
> To start again before you've even stopped.
> Lavinia's no longer one who breathes.
> She's branches and the twigs you twist to wreathes.
> Inanimate but still in need of mending.
> So take her childhood lead and start the bending.

Gary, could ya come out here in me aside?

GARY

(Peeking his head out of the curtain) Can I do that?

JANICE

I'm using me ingenuity.

GARY

Ya alright?

JANICE

To mend, one can't continue to ignore:
One mourns, regards, and then adjusts the chore.

GARY

Was that a rhyme?

JANICE

Plus cleaning could become a change of ways
And not just the degree of mess and craze.

Hold that branch there for me?

(Gary does. Janice starts making a canopy out of the branches.)

If all the chaos here was shaped with order—
Like how the bodies are inside a border—
If a simplicity were part of grandeur,
Perhaps what's loud and grand could be a savior.

GARY

Yeah?

JANICE

If *reverence* and irreverence were both blended
Then it is possible a Fooling could be splendid.

GARY

I could work with that.

JANICE

And if we see the blood as blood and paint,
The art, not gore of it,

GARY

Could make us faint
With awe, not shock, and that becomes a hope.

JANICE

(Holding up her creation)
And therein lies a way for us to cope.

But first things first.

GARY

Gotta deal with the crazy?

SCENE 8

Janice pulls the curtain open, revealing Carol in the same position she was in before the curtain was drawn and finishing her scream out.

CAROL

—OOOOOOOOOOOO.

JANICE

Calm down Carol.

CAROL

Can't breathe.

JANICE

Look at me.

CAROL

Not ha-a-a-pe-ning.

JANICE

Look at the clown. I can do tricks. Woooo!

(Janice does a pratfall to cheer up Carol. It doesn't work.)

CAROL

AHHHHHH.

GARY

Oh Janice, yeah, look at the bad clown Carol.

(Gary tries to juggle and drops things.)

CAROL

(Throwing poo at Gary) AHHHHHH!

JANICE

Hey Gary, did you hear the one about the—

GARY

The maid, the clown and the midwife who walked into a . . .

CAROL

AHHHHHHH!

JANICE

Walked into a . . .

CAROL

AHHHHHHH!

GARY

Look at the . . .

JANICE

Look at the . . .

GARY

Look at the Fooling.

(Gary unties a leg that is above a teeter-totter-like catapult. The leg drops and catapults a severed head across the room where it knocks over an arm that smacks a butt on a corpse that leaps forward and starts a domino of corpses falling to the ground.)

CAROL

(Becoming transfixed) AHHHHHHHHHHHHHhhhhhhhhhh.

(The domino starts a sequence of events, transforming the space into all the things Gary talked about his coup being [though the Rube Goldberg machine should be a theatrical faking of one, that gives the appearance of moments propelled into other moments, but which becomes fantastic—perhaps wonderfully obvious—in its faking]. One after another, increasing in speed and ridiculousness, and crescendoing into a simultaneous and organized chaos, there are miniature bombings, infernos, and floods. The intestines attaching it all are an endless maze of spiderwebs. Corpses pop up in heroic battle poses and crash into other heroes who have popped up: A dead rat with pigeon-pheasant wings glued on it flies by and attacks the cleft chin. Sparks of smoke explode and crescendo into an explosion of an explosion.

Gary runs around, helping it along its way and being part of its creation. Janice and Carol begin to help. Every-thing is present, except for the ensemble of ensembles and the shark. In the end, the wedding canopy, which were Lavinia's branches, springs up, and Janice, as emperor-maid, officiates; and Gary and the handsome corpse as grooms, stand in the center while cannons explode and white and red rose petals fall from the ceiling. At this moment, all the corpses lose their clothes, and all their penises, at the same time, move from right to left [yes really].

All is quiet. They are exhausted from their creation. The pigeon Gary threw up earlier flies in, hovers over Gary, and then poops on him, and flies off.)

EPILOGUE

GARY

I'm gonna get us killed.

JANICE

(Curious about it) I think I'm having a feeling.

GARY

Sort of just dumb isn't it?

JANICE

(Gesturing to the audience) Well some of the court seemed to like it.

GARY

What ya saying, the court's been here from the top?

JANICE

Gotta arrive early to get a good seat for an inauguration. Who'd ya think they were?

GARY

Me imaginary friends.

JANICE

No, that's the court.

GARY

But then it didn't work. Not in the way I visioned it.

JANICE

Well enough.

GARY

But none of them out there ran through the banquet hall naked. And it's all just sort of tragic still.

(Carol exits. The door opens. Screams are heard. It shuts.)

And now we've lost Carol. *(Regarding an audience member)* Plus that person right there got a look on their face like, once they're out of here they're gonna throw the metaphorical poo.

JANICE

Gary, it's really rude to entice a person into a Fooling and then convince them it was a bad idea.

GARY

But it's not the sort of thing that's gonna save the world.

JANICE

Well it was just a first try. We gotta rehearse.

GARY

What, so it can become a routine?

JANICE

Ain't gonna make it better just by hoping, gotta refine it. And we don't got all the pieces yet, we're missing the ensemble of the ensembles, and the shark. And it's clear to me now, it's gotta be bigger than what you said. We need a choir, and a marching band, fireworks, an endless procession of the poor so extravagant it can't be ignored. And women. I WOULD like to see a line of LIVING women kicking all in one direction, symbolizing a revolt, and taking over the world.

GARY

Really?

JANICE

So set up the Fooling from the beginning, while I rally the masses.

GARY

But I wasn't thinking.

JANICE

Ya saying I can't do it?

GARY

Got wrapped up in a feeling. You go out there with the gold laurel they'll kill ya.

JANICE

Well . . . *(Taking the crown off)* Maybe they won't even notice. Being that I'm the type who can finish a job without wearing a bauble.

(Janice throws the crown in the heap of bodies while she exits. As she opens the door, the world screams. The door closes and Gary is alone. Carol enters with a real baby. No matter how the baby responds [sleeps, cries, poops, laughs], the actors play the remaining scene and incorporate the baby into it. This means the end of the play will be played differently every night depending on how the baby responds. Some nights the actors will need to shout over crying. Other times they'll try to comfort it. Sometimes they'll be more quiet to not wake it up. Maybe one night Gary changes it onstage. Another night they might have to sing-song their dialogue to put it to sleep. And, yes, sometimes, it will cry hysterically, as babies do, throughout the entire ending of the play. Be brave enough to let the play be changed. It may be unsentimental, sweet, upsetting, annoying, funny, or all of those things at once. A little improv is okay, but the rule of thumb is to change the action of the dialogue depending on what happens with the baby, rather than to change the dialogue itself [it's written in a way that will give you options].)

CAROL

I did it. I saved the baby.

GARY

Oh, look what ya got there.

CAROL

Turns out it was fine. Except, even though they promised, nobody was looking after it. Or even noticing it.

GARY

So ya brought it here?

CAROL

It's the place ya get it sorted.

GARY

Could be or not.

CAROL

But I made it a shark outfit for the Fooling.

(Gary holds up the baby. It wears a shark onesie.)

GARY

Fast work Carol!

CAROL

I could do more. Sort of have my second wind now.

GARY

Well, how 'bout ya make them cherubim then?

CAROL

Well alright, I'm good with babies.

(Carol sits down on a corpse off to the side and starts sewing wings on severed heads.)

GARY

(Sniffing the baby) Oh, I'll try not to take that personally.

> The sensible theatrical advice
> That's passed through all the genres and the ages
> Is never work with babies dressed as fish.
> Their spontaneity upstages all
> Ideas, maneuvers, and epiphanies.
> A baby's cry is louder than a coup.
> He's like a cameo who steals the show.
> And still to function in a world that don't,
> One must make room for babes, and clowns, and maids,

For cries, for laughter, high-brow and the low,
For casualties and those who are oppressed,
For the experiments not yet expressed.
When life's upstaged by all of its brutality
You show the brutal up with our totality.

(To baby) So here's what's gonna happen. We'll get ya all clean, and then, like Janice says, I'm gonna set it up from the top. So when all the men's penises go from right to left, at the same time, that's your cue, you're gonna enter crawling across the hall with a look on your face like a munching shark who's gonna eat the tragedy of the world. Ya know what I mean?

THE END?